MW01701619

all i have in my hands

kendall a. bell

Maverick Duck Press

www.maverickduckpress.com

First Edition

Cover by Kendall A. Bell

ISBN-13: 979-8-88596-885-0

I. house tornado

II. sun racket

I. house tornado

all i have in my hands

razor wire around bony wrists
and bloodshot confessions over
the smell of dead wood,
in the basement of empty mouse
traps and ugly lamps piled on
an uglier tile floor.
the bad posture, the lambent sun
in glassy eyes, a polio vaccine
scar on the chest. the circular
running to empty parking lots and
the lies that stick out of pockets
and wave in the late winter breeze.
all of these shifting realities in
the wrinkles of knuckles—
grease stained kitchen cabinets
and a fist on the spine that will
not release.

broke off a piece of your terrible secret

left it on a window sill in the kitchen—
stared at the sliver of dark while i
made coffee, while my eyes swelled and
leaked saline. morning brought sun, the
lie glossing over the crispness in the air,
while you steal all of the hot water, the
steam lifting your blame into air ducts,
into the spiderwebbed corners of the ceiling.
goosebumped, i am picking lint from my shirt—
another morning filled with want, this open
wound that never heals.

then suddenly, everything i see's a love letter

hidden in the bunker of a heart
buried under miles of impenetrable
dirt. Then suddenly, everything
becomes a tsunami, the torrent
that wipes everything out, that
leaves only the pages committed to
memory. Suddenly, everything is ink
faded, words that time disappears
at its own discretion. Hearts left
in idle will shatter with neglect.

i never bitched at anyone, i never asked for my heart back

just left it in a bar, on bathroom walls,
on the back of a toilet with a
broken handle, stickers on the door
from bands long gone. seal it in
shellac, in the artificial green
light. paid to come to new york city,
read from the slouch in the back,
gave it up for the two hundredth time
to people who can't spell my name.
tap this vein, there might be something
left keep in your armoire. to crave
an unspoken final word. too fucking shy
to ask for a loaner. ziplock that fucker
and pawn it in some rundown town.

the buzz sounds sweet to me

even under this thunder sky,
milkweed growing through the
cracks in the foundation,
and your always wet shirts
hang from the line—
no random dandelion fuzz,
the birds shit on my car
instead. your hum is the
thrum in my skull, your up
and down scale of sing song
afterglow. *one sour finger,*
pretty as a picture.

a doormat is good honest work

treads deep worn into the
back, pull out pockets
thread thinned and emptied—
your feet are always welcome
here. misaligned, i will stay
crooked for you, a hung over
bird on wine ripe berries.
bootstraps caught in a storm
door, a spill, a spell.
a mouth agape, a moan over
wet brick. some strange angel.

we just drove away into the day

we packed nothing—
some kind of abandonment,
some kind of jail break.
we can hydroplane on this
winter wet, this gray
swallows the trail behind us.
knots undone, and frayed thread
over old brick covered in
bird shit. one last surgery to
save both patients. one last iv
drip in an antiseptic room.
our stitches are bleeding,
and we don't know where to go
to disappear.

that firepile's your home

that sore kneecap bend,
a pinch and twist in the
thick evening, your basket
full of dirty clothes and
shredded purple hearts—
the sparrows dive bomb the
gutters, push through the
hyper crowd twitching on a
wire. braid her hair in a
ball of confusion, this sad
song on an old radio with a
tinny speaker. *i rush to
wait where the pavement
starts to crack.* she's the
flicker in the punch of night.

i forget what it's like to be kissing in the middle of a terrible dream

some b movie on the television cranked to
irritate from rooms away, and i am roads
full of potholes and abandoned hubcaps.
nothing worthwhile comes when the lights
make your eyes red, when your cherry mouth
is glued shut. i writhe through winter,
fill my split chest with bees and sugar.
vows are just a sentimental sickness left
to spread—some half-assed effort, some
sore hip and yellowed bruises stretched
like a flood. *you have to look close to*
see what this disease has done to me.

love is half blast and half vacant

and dreams escape through door cracks,
run down dirt lined gutters to tumble
into thistle and red dirt. your face
in the thin pond ice. your face is a
chalk drawn heart on the black wall,
is a butterfly gone to mexico. hands
are empty oven mitts, are winter dry
and uncoupled. our rumble water boil,
wrap up in fresnel light over high
grass with sleeping baby bunnies and
field mice. video sync dream terrain,
wake me up hungry, wake me up wild.
our bodies have weight and have motion.

possible dust clouds

possible contaminated drinking water,
a forbearing in muddied footprints.
possible held breath, possible mercury
in the veins—milk eyed glaze and the
howl over mountains and treetops.
possible termites in elbows, possible
derecho through the center of town—
a clear out, and the dial back into
centuries buried under schoolyard
playgrounds and metal blast site
skeletons. possible drought vagabond
tent camps, possible ash interred endings.

i've been caught with red hands

everything on me is a blush,
is the frozen heartbeat left
as a sunrise over a rooftop,
how this bloat is insistent
reminder—the broken insides
of a grandfather clock. the
heavy rope over a dam, body
death on display. they will
discard me like rusted locks,
my pockets filled with fig
bars and broken cigarettes,
with ravenous intention—
when i'm free from me
you'll hear me in the wind.

sunshine isn't strychnine

it only feels like death burned
into cells, the strident blast
that sends you to retreat under
blankets, in rooms filled with
somber reminders and burned out
lightbulbs. pull down the felt
hearts in the windows, and carry
off the displays of love to the
basement. it smells like unread
novels and dryer sheets down
here. you can survive a nuclear
winter in this icebox with a day
bed, with an arsenal of batteries
and all of your unused notebooks.
no one was going to read your
dipshit rambling anyway, and your
heart is a shaky blue can—
wide awake and sun spilled.

you're so tall, it's like i climb a waterfall

nothing to grab to keep me from
complete collapse, a raincloud
to follow, to drown, to imprison
under your tyrant reign. stare
into multiplex vortex, these nights
are a barren tree, a glass of melted
ice cubes, a taste of freezer frost
and abandoned ice cream containers.
sing for me—*never was a baritone*
til' you stepped in. a door frame
dance to seduce, arms never stretched
far enough to pull down the shades,
to steer you away from thick vines
and the dirt under your nails.
baked bread fresh, an unblemished thing.
nothing ever spoiled on me.

i built a tower in my bones

it's all backward clocks and the thud
of heartbeats against cracking mortar,
a clogged sink, smeared fingerprints
along spider-cracked porcelain. kept
in the bone prison is one thousand
spider corpses, a tarnished locket—
memory is dead dog hair under your
desk, the tick, tick, tick of moments
ready to send the structure to ruin.
voices loiter in your skin. clear cut
through this broken greenhouse mausoleum.

i was born with a sad song in my mouth

a dirge, a folk song where
death is verse-chorus-verse.
i have hummed it like a hymn
from the day i could round
my mouth, on the walk home
alone from excommunication—
this isn't candyland,
it's musical chairs and i am
on the floor with ankles
twisted under my legs, with
penny candy scattered around
the fragmented leavings of a
child. *life is unkind 'til it*
burns up your memories.

i'm so sorry i'm cardiac baggage

and my bad time management that
strands us in another dormant
morning. these country roads are
always so fucked, and we pass
dilapidated barns and the stench
of invisible passive—an endless
drive to nowhere, to muddy fields,
mired in this late morning hunger,
and internet girlfriends, hard
lessons the easy way. making me
make plans is the definition of a
breakdown, a letdown. *is everything
fading away?*

it's moonshine from cactus

shitfaced in the sand,
a drunk dial,
the sideways gaze into
dying stars and the
full moon over the wail
of stray dogs and you,
stumbling over your own
rubber limbs.
a skinnydip—my shipwreck
body stays behind,
your full gut laugh echoes
over ripples and empty bottles,
your night ocean hair
a-shine with sheen.

II. sun racket

water hangs in the air like you stayed

but you found a delete button,
a kitchen knife,
the cover of snow flurries
and broken down boxes to barricade
the windows at the sun's break.
you burned up books and river beds,
circled your own drain and pooled
in the corners, knees to chest.
your coyote sunset, your forest backyard—
you didn't bother to scream
or leave the radio on some classic rock
station. your dropped phone call mind,
fishing for reason, a cloud to push aside.
airborne, *where the kisses fly.*

bones were made to be broken

herding goats over uneven rocks
and the remains of dead trees,
watch out for the random piles
of shit, for the lost balance,
the end of another stupid summer.
something else to navigate in
the hip ache, in the crunch of
the brittle feathers scattered
around dried out milkweed. send
anonymous poems—listen for the
hairline fractures. it's the
love notes left near the park
bench, we bite our heavy tongues,
set ourselves up for collision
in the knee deep snap of evening.

dancing with scissors, our bones full of wishes

sweet nothings in a fruit bowl under
the kitchen window heat, every peach
bruised and fragile like a sand dune
under the tide. dreams are a lightning
storm, are the shreds of grass dragged
in from wet shoes. all of our sad-eyed
lament piled against the back door—
it counts painstaking days, the thrill
of disappearance in hurricane season.
we are the cracked enamel of teeth,
the doze off under the swarm of gnats
and sticky skin. *we fill each other's*
arms, you wanna wish higher, lose control.

sweet nothing, sweet dreams

the space in front of the heater
isn't big enough to share—
gathered dreams bulge from a
cedar chest, all of our sweet
nothings carried off to muddied
baseball fields, underneath cars
still covered in the last snow.
a soundless serenade, we repose
in the bedroom's chill, find one
more day to bury like a bassinet—
pencil mark the white lies behind
the daybed, dust mites and polar
nights. the howl of wind through
a dryer vent, our long dead garden.
sweet nothing, sweet dreams.

for today i've arranged to be just enough deranged

hacking down dying lilac bushes in sunday
heat. this body ache, like one thousand
kidney punches—the wake stupor and walls
and floors like a pinball machine. your
gravel kisses and classic horror movie
retreats. the front door's open—wave to
the landscapers, wave to the monarch in
the garden. the boredom is a face slap,
is the upside down sink into the moss.
find me under the steps, empty bottles
of wine at my feet and my pizza cheese
burnt tongue. i dance alone. i don't
dance at all. *what can i tell you that*
you'll believe?

these dog days always leave me with a stomach ache

emptied containers and the crumbs of
nacho chips, stray lettuce strands
and chatter from your ridiculous
headphones. it will get hotter and
i'll still skim a dull blade between
beads of sweat to find impossible
relief. *i wanna go away somewhere* is
your endless refrain, and somewhere
is always nowhere, and nowhere is
this house in a death throe, is our
bodies and the symphony of new cracks.
we're always starving for a getaway,
we're always so fucking bored. *just*
keep telling me this is life and we
didn't miss it.

junkie hearts are broken

ice-laid, this jagged terrain leaves
veins bulging, a collar crumb dusted.
spread out on the uneven carpet in
the company of dull blades, stench of
neglect, of unremedied brain rot.
a spell, a snap, a stinging silence.
call it cranial impact. call it ripped
out wires dangled over a gas oven.
sell copper for blood rush, to deal in
a slideshow of gradient colors in dusk.
i lost every friend i ever made,
but i like it too much.

we're floating on inflatable hope

our fingers over the air tube,
our fingers are liars, are the
sign of a sunnyside up sun that
is holding a middle finger behind
its back. build that book fortress
and don't spill your expensive tea
leaves on the fucking kitchen mat.
we're that robin outside the office
window singing like a dumbass while
the dark covers this boring town.
gps will send us to the shore to
fade in a briny fog, the keeper of
my pathetic dream. *only you can see*
eden through the blizzard.

a glimmer of the future made this winter even crueler

the gently used napkins scattered over
your desk, harbor freight and bronze
suitcase locks on bird feeders, the
squirrels are living better than us.
soil and sand, some things can't grow
in impenetrable ground. a break in the
cold snap—crocuses and daffodils crest
the surface, weeds grab harder than
any fruit. scatter the remnants of a
harvest like abandon. *a buzzing like*
panic made this whole spring kind of manic.

it's why i piss and moan, it's why i can't go home

stranded on the beach with jagged
slippershell violence, these days are
wet dog footprints, are the leaf pile
against a rotting fence. black mold
around the eyes, principles like the
scattered crumbs on your dresser—
fake ass virtue and you can't take all
of your shit with you when it's nothing
but ash. wake up and overdose on
liquid crack, knock back all of your
stale cigarettes under cloud cover and
the swoop of fungus gnats. the circle
of handmaids are forming, this cruelty
control. *hard water down your throat,*
down your back.

our future together

the shed finally collapses after
a bomb cyclone. white bikini sand
and burn through tacky sunblock
skin. crooked spines in the aerial
carnival, we watch the last sunset
in a coat of shivers. watches set
to a permanent high noon. planes
collide, then firestorm, then the
shipwreck in the gulf of stupid
fucking name changes. another hour
spent watching cancer frauds cry
after they're caught. nails in the
driveway to keep out the solicitors.
our secret knock, our neon halo in
the superunknown.

fireworks for you in the ozone snow

and the cries of frightened dogs,
our undeterred eyes over the river,
and our pneumonia shivers, crusted
flatland under foot. *you rub your*
hands together – sparks fly.
we watch promises fly into a
shooting star. our hamster wheel
minds, the uncontrollable spinning.
side by side is still a mountain climb.
we're just a little lonely.

you messing with my head makes a terrible noise

screech owls over night quiet
and coffee stained napkins
scrawled with bad poetry,
with worse love notes.
this chewing tobacco, yellow-
jugged juice. the humiliation
in technicolor, over smeared
screens. clean dreams, downcast
eyes—my kingdom for temporary
deafness, my dumbass heart all
revved and volatile. wrapped
in pastel, spring curtains and
pollinated. *you are whizzing*
past my ears.

could you ever live in a body?

all nerve endings and rivers of blood.
all conflict and screaming. this body
is always ready for mutiny, for the
slash and burn. *could you ever really*
live in a house? it will forget you,
its jagged edges and radon time bombs
set to burst. pleasure becomes a kind
of dementia, a memory lost under the
baseboard heat. the slowest waltz to
the horizon. *i feel almost everything*.

eyeshine to devastation

and something hidden in the snow
beneath this tent. the moon turns
a disapproving eye to my guilty
mouth, dusted with beignet sugar
and thick with lies. twist into a
rubberband, steal from my furnace
body—the mountains stay hungry,
the mountains turn red with rising
temper. this shut down vocabulary,
conflict resolution via skin trade,
then it's dusting for fingerprints,
it's frost lungs baying into black.
your whiteboard brain, wiped clean.
dreams in puzzle pieces, misshapen.

i left my heart on a frozen sidewalk

preserved for the taking,
still warm and ready to
haunt the next rib cage
to encase it. kicked out
onto the rain slicked
driveway to be carried
off by a stray dog. half
a shell of former selves—
no takers, a beheaded
mailbox to rust in the
grass. the subsequent
solitude fits like the
old flannel in your closet,
worn soft and slowly
thinned, *isn't this a*
pretty fall? this dark sky
that settles over you,
this vertigo before black.

i think god dripped you out of a sunbeam

and my atheist hands caught all of your
yellow bright. your velvet inches, some
distant perched call—i think you grew me
out of the dirt, your cowbird scratches
over window sills. something to keep on
a cutting board in the shadow of an oven
hood. hammock hearts and honey glaze,
we were made for bowing sofas and the
bent back aftermath. our call and answer
fearless naked window gaze. you pulled
me out of a church, to worship you.

it sounds like thunder in here

and the roads are sleet slick,
a carrier to telephone poles
and the endless spin in the head.
everything rumbles like destruction,
like the boom of collision on black
winter mornings. turn down the sound
on the tv—it's the same reruns every
night, the death replay, the unending
ads peer into our corpse flesh.
there's a pill for everything,
washed down with nanoplastics and
stale shortbread biscuits.
forever, unsettled dust.

III. moonlight concessions

i think you know the whole thing's a damn shame

rotting fruit in a wooden bowl
fruit flies circle and swoop
a slip on the frozen spot
under the gutter that puddles
bone snap and arthritis radiates
who gets to stumble upon us?
rigor mortis and permanent gape
head full of flowers
this is no fucking golden age
the way it breaks apart like
shorelines and gets swallowed
it lingers like a spell
eggshells are covering the floor
my shaky gait
your mislaid honey traps
soft spots in the walls cave in

how did i love a breaking thing?

everything frayed and spooled in a
pile over an uncomfortable couch,
filled with nostalgia for people
who hate you. it's the bitter taste
of cyanide, the tremors that leave
fingertips bent and useless.
door knocks are deserters—
the broken screen door on its side
on the grass, a mournful howl in
the distance. *i only wanted the spark.*
i only wanted your hearts.

one more somnambulist year

ambition packed away in blue containers
under the squint of daylight, lungs
rusting under showerhead drips. it all
blends together in a bag of threats—
glued to that goddamn chair on the dark
web in search of an elusive, idyllic
bullshit lie you've been served. beach
hobo life, your sun blistered bliss,
seaweed in your hair, pink and filled
with tiny clamshells. what you chase at
night will haunt you in the day.

drugstore drastic

these injections and pills,
anything to keep us vertical,
our foul mouths and chapped elbows—
break a window and take what you need
before the police is militarized.
no one is throwing eggs on mischief
night, not at these fucking prices.
we're all too sober now to be numb,
too filled with dread and helplessness.
stockpile blood pressure meds and chase
them with the last bottle of corona in
your basement. sit in the glow of your
new florescent lights. find that mouse
corpse while you spin scratchy old vinyl.
we all have concessions to make under the
cool tree, these branches are tendrils,
keep us tied to this town of dirt.

i feel broken and miles away

someone's overturned trash can
pushed down the rain slicked
road, landing over a leaf pile
and days old dog shit. count the
lives i've shed on one hand—
snake skins decomposed and fed
to the ground, and there is no
return, no strong arm to pull me
back in. square peg, round hole—
second verse, same as the first,
a neck slumped and shadowed over
river water. i can wash up on any
shore and be a shoulder shrug.
let the brain bells ring again.

dead is next door

it knocks like an engine,
a debbie downer on steroids,
cuts a hole in the fence
and leaves empty whiskey
bottles next to your shed.
you lousy mentor.
you dead weight in cargo shorts.
bead me a necklace from the
apple seeds i spit at your feet.
limbs disjointed and left in
limbo. your motel room filled
with empty lube bottles and
stale pizza crust. rosacea and
your autism self diagnosis—
you lousy empath.

we hover blurry and glassy eyed

and i'm tired of being the only one
to put away the goddamned dishes,
cabinets left open for house flies
and ceiling fan dust bunnies.
a pall hangs over a celebration—
we don't know how to do dignified,
sweatpants and condensation rings
burned into end tables and ten year
old magazines we always forget to
recycle. your puny savings blown,
this thunderstorm is a drive-in
theater, and we wait for alerts on
our phones to head for the basement,
tornadoes hungry for our roof.
a lover on a night with no moon.

under the horny sun of july

we swelter and bend like tulips
under a hostile breeze, keep our
heavy breath in mason jars, the
neighbors poking squinted eyes
through dirty blinds. our chaos
is a crackling firepit, a pair
of stilettos under a dry spigot.
summer theater for the puritans,
the low buzz of lawnmowers and
ten thousand miles of moonscape—
we shed barriers like snakes.

how much for a life you don't despise

a blistered hand and pinked skin,
this sun slaps you like a dog.
a notebook full of grievances,
barter for the rest of your life.
the clutter of disgust crowds you,
this weird shaped foundation, all
crabgrass and buried coffee cans
with dead birds. your jar of dust
dulled quarters can't bail you out
of this life. serenity threw eggs
at your house, stole all of the
strawberries from your garden.
water for a thirst you can't fight.

the heart of missing you

sun crisped, and blisters scream,
docks are made for misery,
and a swim is a catastrophe
when you never learned to even
float, to tread water.
a sullen apple rotting in the dirt,
skin too tough to peel back,
this green screen in a dry county,
breaking dead tree fingers over
mud caked shoe grooves—
an expert at meandering in a void.
lake water ripples, and i am a
shipwreck, so full of rotted wood
and longing, a gutted fish.

today i want to walk away

tear a hole in the clouds,
two feet towards reverse
and the sky is temptation,
the sky is a torn parachute
caught in a painting—
a body becomes used to the
descent, a stomach becomes
a trampoline, so much bloat.
tied to phantom skin trade
and old refrains that hum
in the walls like a hornet
nest. a belly full of sour
milk, full of bully taunts.
nothing helps me fall.
nothing helps me float.

this is the last curse

sparrow feathers and plucked blonde
hair mingled with plaintive moans
over the break of raindrops on the
scuffed trash can. backward guitar
strokes and fever sweat—your body
is rejecting this attempt to heal.
your body is a heckler that sits
on a brick wall across the street,
fist wags and stink eyed stares.
below sea level, and swamp lit stars
bear down in the boggy stench.
skeletal evidence in the firepit,
muscle death and blood soaked sheets,
and i'm not going home now.

i wake up feeling fragile

all ankles and bent spine—
the sunlight hasn't been born yet,
and a book is a good distraction.
the pills i forget to take on purpose,
or maybe it's the misfire of brain cells
that sends me to a loop, to a dust layered
glass of water, barely lukewarm, and there
aren't enough diversions from the frost
on your shoulders, from the way headlights
are a head-on collision—
a belly full of some kind of sickness,
or maybe sky high ordinary is an open hand
slap, or the scribbled notes and post mortem
instructions, a thousand knees in the back.
in a cleaner light, it's ok.

Kendall A. Bell's poetry has been most recently published in As It Ought To Be and First Literary Review-East. He was nominated for Sundress Publications' Best of the Net collection seven times. He is the author of five full length collections, "The Roads Don't Love You" (2018), "the forced hush of quiet" (2019), "the shallows" (2022), "all of this bruising" (2024), "all i have in my hands" (2025), and 37 chapbooks, the latest being "The Contortionist". He is the publisher/editor of Maverick Duck Press and editor and founder of Chantarelle's Notebook. His chapbooks are available through Maverick Duck Press. He lives in Southern New Jersey.

Made in the USA
Middletown, DE
31 May 2025

76178478R10035